know your pet

HAMSTERS

Anna and Michael Sproule

The Bookwright Press
New York · 1988

Know Your Pet

Cats   Rabbits
Dogs   Hamsters

First published in the
United States in 1988 by
The Bookwright Press
387 Park Avenue South
New York, NY 10016

First published in 1988 by
Wayland (Publishers) Limited,
61 Western Road, Hove,
East Sussex, BN3 1JD, England.

Library of Congress Cataloging-in-Publication Data

Sproule, Anna
    Know your pet hamsters/by Anna & Michael Sproule
        p.   cm. — (Know your pet series)
    Bibliography: p.
    Includes index.
    Summary: Offers tips on how to keep a hamster in
your home, discussing the care, feeding, breeding,
exercise, equipment, and how to enter your hamster in a
pet show.
    ISBN 0-531-18216-9
    1. Golden hamsters as pets — Juvenile literature.
[1. Hamsters.] I. Sproule, Michael. II. Title. III. Series.
SF459.H3S67   1988
    636'.93233—dc 19   87-34200
                                        CIP
                                        AC

Designed and produced by BLA Publishing
Limited, East Grinstead, Sussex, England.

A member of the Ling Kee Group
LONDON · HONG KONG · TAIPEI · SINGAPORE · NEW YORK

Photographic credits

t = top, b = bottom, l = left, r = right

cover: Chris Fairclough Picture Library

8, 9t, 9b, 12, 13 Chris Fairclough Picture Library; 16,
18 Trevor Hill; 19, 20, 21t, 21b, 22, 23, 24t, 24b, 25, 26,
30t, 30b, 31 Chris Fairclough Picture Library;
32 Frank Lane; 33 Bruce Colman Limited; 35, 36, 37,
38t, 38b, 39, 40; Chris Fairclough Picture Library

Illustrations by Derick Bown/Linden Artists;
and Steve Lings/Linden Artists
Printed in Italy by G. Canale & C.S.p.A. – Turin

**Cover: Like all hamsters, the Golden
Hamster uses its front paws like
hands to hold its food. Descendants
from a single family of Syrian
hamsters, Golden Hamsters are now
the most popular and widely kept of
the breeds.**

**Title page: Although hamsters are solitary
by nature and can be aggressive
to each other, once tame they
make friendly pets.**

Contents

Note to the Reader

In this book there are some words in the text which are printed in **bold** type. This shows that the word is listed in the glossary on page 44. The glossary gives a brief explanation of words which may be new to you.

Introduction

If you have not had a pet before, it is a good idea to start with something small. A hamster makes a good first pet. Hamsters are clean animals and take up very little space. They are easy to handle and fun to watch.

Having pets at home

There are many things you have to think about before you decide to get a hamster. You must make sure that the other people in your home will welcome it. Is there a place for the cage to go? Are there other animals in your house that could frighten or harm the hamster? Most important of all, are you quite sure that you would be able to care for your pet?

You need to know how much it will cost to feed your hamster and what problems there may be. This book will help you, but try to learn more about any pitfalls by talking to a friend who has a hamster.

▼ This boy has just brought his hamster home from the pet shop. Is the cage going to be large enough for his pet? Where will he keep the cage? Has he bought the right kind of exercise wheel? There are many problems for the pet owner to solve.

► This hamster is gnawing away at a thin plastic container. Hamsters will gnaw at anything you give them. But thin plastic things are dangerous. A splinter of the plastic could stick in the hamster's pouch. This might cause an injury, and then your pet would get sick.

▼ Hamsters love to be handled. Once your pet has settled down in its new home, it will soon become friendly. Then you can play with it gently several times a day. But hold it carefully and avoid sudden actions.

Caring for your pet

Remember that pets are not toys. They are living creatures, which need an owner's loving care to keep them well and happy.

Hamsters are **solitary** animals, and your pet will live on its own in the cage you provide. The cage will be the hamster's world, so you must give it as large a cage as possible. You will need to keep the cage interesting and give the hamster a chance to move about freely. Hamsters quickly become bored and restless if they do not get enough exercise.

Besides giving your hamster food and water, you must always keep the cage clean. You will have to do these things without fail for all the hamster's life. Hamsters live for about two years, and sometimes a little longer.

In return, your pet will give you hours of fun and interest. By watching it closely, you will get to know it as well as you know your friends.

About hamsters

Hamsters are members of a group of animals called **rodents**. Other rodents include rats, mice and gerbils. The word "rodent" comes from a Latin word meaning "to gnaw." All rodents have sharp front teeth, called **incisors**, and hamsters will use these to gnaw almost anything. This means that you must take care in choosing a cage, which should be made of hard wood or metal.

Hamsters are **herbivores**, which means that they eat only plant food. In the wild they live on grain and seeds, roots and fruit. They need to keep their teeth sharp and strong. For this reason they should be given kinds of food which they can hold in their claws and gnaw.

Hoarders

The hamster gets its name from a German word hamstern, which means "to hoard." It has the **instinct** to store food in its cheek pouches, taking the food back to its store to eat later. These pouches are very large. You will get a surprise the first time you see a hamster with its pouches full.

In the wild, hamsters live in deep **burrows** and store their food there. Your pet hamster will want to store its food, and there must be a place in the cage where it can do this.

▶ The Golden Hamster comes from the Syrian Desert in the Middle East. The days are very hot and the nights are cold. So hamsters sleep during the day in burrows away from the heat of the desert sun. In the cool of the evening they come out and hunt for food. They roam around looking for seeds and greenstuff. They collect the food in their pouches. Back in the burrow they put the food in a special food store.

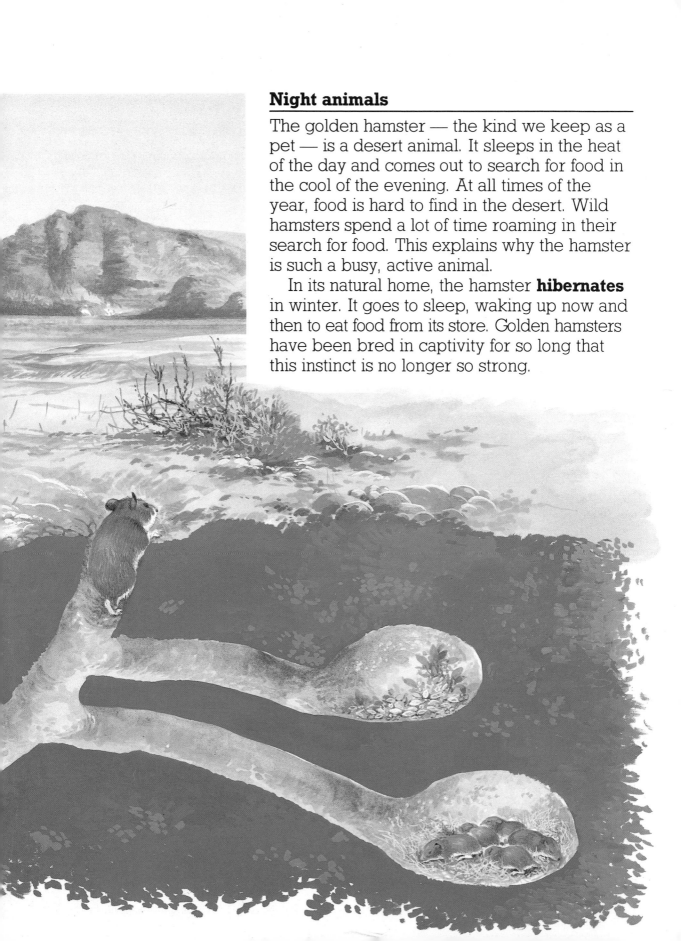

Night animals

The golden hamster — the kind we keep as a pet — is a desert animal. It sleeps in the heat of the day and comes out to search for food in the cool of the evening. At all times of the year, food is hard to find in the desert. Wild hamsters spend a lot of time roaming in their search for food. This explains why the hamster is such a busy, active animal.

In its natural home, the hamster **hibernates** in winter. It goes to sleep, waking up now and then to eat food from its store. Golden hamsters have been bred in captivity for so long that this instinct is no longer so strong.

The twentieth-century pet

Golden hamsters have been kept as pets for only about fifty years. Until about 1930, they were mystery animals. Only a few had been seen in the western world, and some experts thought that the species had died out.

The golden hamster

All kinds of hamsters have large pouches in their cheeks and live in deep burrows. The golden hamster is just one of a large group of hamsters. Its natural home is in the Middle East, and every golden hamster brought from the wild was found there in Syria. It was first discovered in 1839 by an Englishman, George Waterhouse. Around 1880, another Englishman, James Skene, brought some hamsters back to England. These were bred in captivity, but after 30 years the line died out. Everyone forgot about the golden hamster until 1930. Then, Dr. Israel Aharoni, a zoologist, discovered a nest of eight in Syria. Three of these — one male and two females — were bred from in captivity. All the pet hamsters in the world are descended from these three animals.

▲ Hamsters have round, plump bodies and colorful coats. Some hamsters have pink eyes, but most of them have eyes that are jet black and shiny. They use their front paws, each of which has four fingers, in much the same way that we use our hands.

◄ Some varieties of hamsters have glossy coats that shine like satin or silk. All hamsters with this kind of coat are called satins.

Breeding habits

A **litter** of hamsters is born only 16 days after the parents have mated. A litter usually numbers about seven, though it may be only three or as many as sixteen. When about four weeks old, the young hamsters can look after themselves and the mother is ready to mate again. You can figure from this that a female, if free to mate, could have fifty or more young each year. The female offspring could start mating at about ten weeks, and each one could produce another fifty young in a year.

This explains why the keeping of hamsters as pets has spread so quickly. It also explains why **selective breeding** — breeding from very carefully chosen pairs to bring out different features — has resulted in so many different color varieties. It could mean something else as well. If too many pet hamsters escaped and bred, the twentieth-century pet could become a twentieth-century pest!

► The hamster seen playing in this picture is known as the Angora or Longhaired variety. It was first bred in the United States around 1970. Longhaired hamsters need to be groomed daily to prevent their long hair from becoming matted.

A home for your hamster

Your hamster will spend all its life in the cage you give it. This means that its home must be large enough to contain sleeping quarters, a feeding area and room for running around.

First you must decide where the cage is to go. Hamsters like to be in a light place, but they do not like direct sunlight. They also like to be warm, but not too warm.

What kind of cage?

Hamsters are great escapers. They are experts at finding their way through any gap, so the cage must be escape-proof. If there is a door, it should fit tightly and not be too small. You must be able to take your pet out and put it back easily. Some cages have top sections that lift off, and this makes handling and cleaning easier.

▼ **Half the fun of keeping a hamster is the pleasure you get from giving your pet a good home to live in. Make sure that your hamster has plenty of room to move around in, and plenty of things to do. Then you will have all the more fun watching your pet. See page 18 for a collection of toys.**

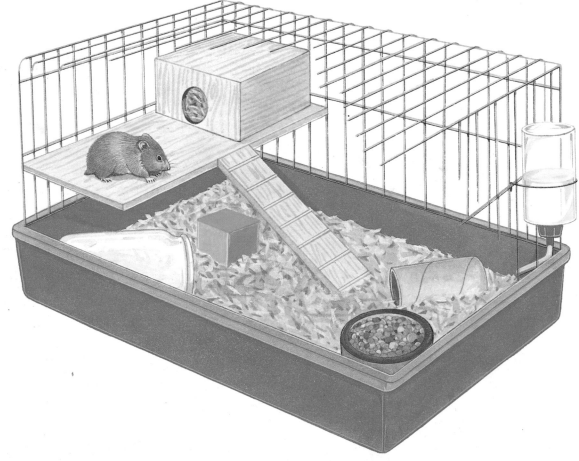

► Golden hamsters like to nest and sleep during the day. There should be a separate nesting box in the cage, with soft hay for bedding. The box should have a lid so you can look inside and change the hay from time to time.

▼ Never let your hamster go short of water. You can hang a drip-feed drinking water bottle on the outside of the cage. Keep the spout clear of the litter on the floor of the cage. Put fresh water in the bottle each day.

It would be difficult to make an escape-proof cage yourself, so you must buy one. There are many sizes and shapes, but a good size would be 75 cm × 40 cm (30 in × 16 in), floor area, and about 40 cm (16 in) high. Most modern cages are made of metal, with a hard plastic base. Some have floors that slide out for cleaning.

There should also be a nesting box. This is often fixed to the side of the cage with a ladder up to it. The top should come off the nesting box for cleaning.

Part of the floor of the cage should be kept as the feeding area, with a food bowl, and, nearby, a plastic drip-feed drinking bottle. Your hamster also needs a "play area" where it can exercise.

What goes in the cage?

The best kind of **litter** for the floor of the cage is sawdust, but a mixture of dried peat and sand may also be used. You will also need to provide bedding which your pet will use to make its nest. Use fresh hay if you can, but clean shredded paper or wood shavings will do very well. Do not use any plastic materials, or paper that has been printed on.

Choosing your hamster

Here are two pieces of advice for when you go to the pet shop to buy your hamster! Take someone with you to help you choose, and allow plenty of time. It is best to go with one of your parents or with an adult who knows about hamsters. There may be many different ones to choose from. If you do not see one you really like, wait for another day and try other shops.

The signs to look for

You should buy your hamster when it is between six and ten weeks old. At that age it will be able to look after itself but will be young enough to get used to a new home. You will have to decide whether you want a male or a female. Unless you intend to breed hamsters, it does not really matter.

▼ Most large pet shops will have a good selection of hamsters for you to choose from. Look at each hamster carefully and watch how it behaves. When you see one you like, ask if you can handle it.

When you have seen one you like, watch it closely in its cage. It should be bright-eyed and alert. The coat should be smooth and glossy, with no cuts, sores or bald patches. Ask the pet-shop assistant to show you the coat on the animal's stomach, and under its tail. Do not consider a hamster that looks dirty. If you are interested in buying, then ask if you can handle the one you like.

Handling hamsters

Hamsters are shy animals and panic easily. When you go to pick one up, move slowly and make sure the hamster can see what you are doing. If you are worried about being bitten, wear gloves — but a young hamster's bite is not really painful and is quite harmless.

Hamsters have poor eyesight but a good sense of smell. Before you pick a hamster up for the first time, put your gently-closed fist forward and let it smell your hand. Speak very quietly to it, stroking gently. When it has had a chance to get used to you, pick it up in both hands as shown in the picture.

▲ When you pick up a hamster, make your movements slow and gentle. Make a cup with your hands so that the hamster will feel safe and warm inside them.

17

Making your hamster happy

A healthy hamster is a busy, exploring animal. It is active in the evening and at night. You should never try to persuade a hamster to play when it wants to sleep. When you first take your pet home, the shock may make it go to sleep for a time. Just let it sleep. When evening comes, it will wake up and be ready to look around its new home.

Playtime!

Hamsters like to have a variety of things to do. You can buy hamster toys at any pet shop, but it is cheaper and more fun to think up your own. Hamsters like tunnels and tube-shaped objects. The cardboard tubes from toilet rolls and kitchen towels will give your pet endless fun. Hamsters also enjoy climbing. If there is room in the cage, you could make an "adventure playground" out of ladders and twigs.

Hamsters also need things to gnaw. Wooden spools and small blocks of wood are ideal, but do not give it anything painted or made of plastic.

▲ A collection of toys and objects in the cage keeps your hamster busy and interested. Wooden spools, cardboard tubes and pieces of wood all make good toys. Look among some old toys and see if you can find something that will keep your hamster active.

◄ The exercise wheel is very important for your hamster. If you can do so, give your hamster a large solid wheel like the one shown in the picture. This kind of wheel is better than a wheel made of metal wire, in which the hamster can catch its claws in the gaps.

▲ Hamsters like climbing ladders. Ask your pet shop for the right kind of ladder. It should be made of metal, hard wood or hard plastic. If it is a plastic ladder make sure your pet does not try gnawing it.

Exercise

In the wild, hamsters have to search far and wide for food. As pets, they do not need to, but they must have some kind of exercise.

You can buy an exercise wheel inside which the hamster can keep running. Make sure it is one designed for hamsters. Those for mice and gerbils are too small. There should be no axle running through the middle, as this can damage the hamster's coat and cause sores. The rim of the wheel should be solid, so that there is no danger of the hamster's catching its claws.

The slight noise that exercise wheels make can be cut down with oiling. Use olive oil or vegetable oil for safety. Even then the exercise wheel will still make some noise. That is one reason why you should not keep the cage in your bedroom. The time for your sleep is just the time for your hamster's nightly run!

Feeding hamsters

Hamsters begin to get active in the evening, and that is a good time for the daily feeding. If you feed your hamster at a regular time each day it will come to the front of the cage to greet you when you bring its food bowl.

What kind of food?

In the wild, golden hamsters feed on seeds, roots and fruit. It is easy to provide this sort of **diet** at home, or you can buy ready-made "hamster mix" at the pet shop. If you do this, you should add other things to give a balanced diet.

You can make your own home-made mix quite easily. Use unsweetened breakfast cereal, broken up sugar-free unsalted crackers, rolled oats and crumbled bread. Most hamsters prefer their food dry, but some like it made into a mash with a little milk. If you make a mash, use just enough milk to bind the mix together.

▼ Hamsters like a mixture of foods, such as slices of fruit and cheese, and seeds. After nibbling some greenstuff, this hamster will pouch the rest of the food and take it to the food store to be eaten later.

▲ Hamsters like to sit up on their hind legs when taking food. They balance perfectly, and use their front paws as hands to hold the food.

Whether you buy the food or make it up yourself you can add other things that hamsters like. They enjoy eating grapes and raisins, pieces of apple and pear, vegetables such as celery and lettuce, and even young, fresh dandelion leaves. They also enjoy carrots, but they should not have these too often as they stain the coat. Do not give your hamster salted nuts or potato chips, chocolates or oranges.

Keeping clean

If you have pets, **hygiene** is very important. You should wash your hands before and after feeding your hamster. The food bowl must be cleaned each day, and vegetables and fruit should be washed under the faucet.

Hamsters are untidy eaters. They leave food around in their cages, and this must be cleaned out before it goes moldy or attracts flies.

Another hygiene problem is caused by the hamster's hoarding instinct. You cannot keep this from happening, but it can cause the hamster's "larder" to smell. If wet food is stored there, the cage may get rusty. Inspect the "larder" every day and remove anything that seems to be going bad. But do not disturb this stored food more than you have to.

▶ Hamsters enjoy nibbling carrots and other root vegetables. This animal's cheek pouches are full. There is a fold of skin inside the cheeks where food can be stored. The cheek pouch is really a kind of carrying bag.

Caring for your hamster

Hamsters live on their own in the wild, but they enjoy human company. They learn to recognize their owners' voices. They like playing and being spoken to and stroked. When you take your pet out of its cage and let it play on your arms and shoulders, this makes its life more interesting.

Exploring

The key to taming a hamster is to take things slowly. The hamster has to learn that there is no danger, and that it can have some fun by climbing over you. Start by stroking it after it has finished its meal. Let it get used to the smell and feel of your hands. After a while, pick it up in your cupped hands as shown on page 17. Do no more than this for a few days until it has begun to trust you.

▼ Do not expect your new pet to climb up your arm right away. First it must get used to being high off the ground. Soon this hamster will start to explore up the owner's arm. Then the other arm can be used to protect it from falling.

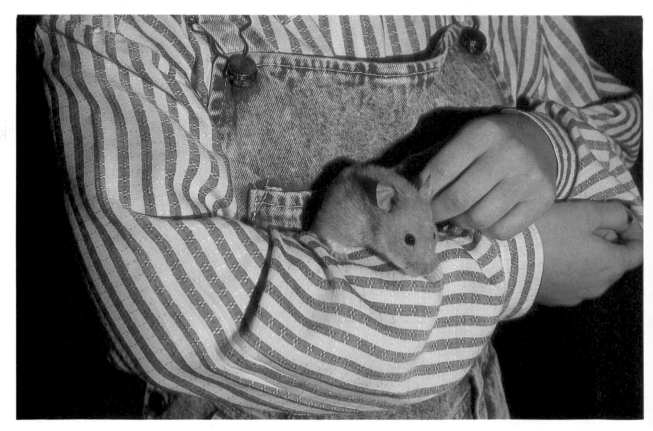

Next, make a "bridge" with your upturned hands and let the hamster move from one arm to the other. Hamsters lose their balance easily, so you should be ready to catch your pet if it slips. Once it begins to explore your arms and shoulders it is safer, because it can cling to your clothes. Do not be surprised if it wants to explore inside your sleeve or down your neck!

Escape!

It is best not to set your hamster free to explore the room. If you do, it is sure to hide under the furniture, or find a hole where it can get under the floorboards.

If it does escape and hide, the best thing to do is to tempt it back with a baited jar. Find a tall jar like those used for bottling fruit, and put some bedding inside. Place a few tidbits of food inside and leave it overnight. The chances are that in the morning you will find that the hamster has been tempted into the jar by the bait, but cannot grip the glass to climb out again. But be careful! It will be frightened and must be left alone in its cage to recover.

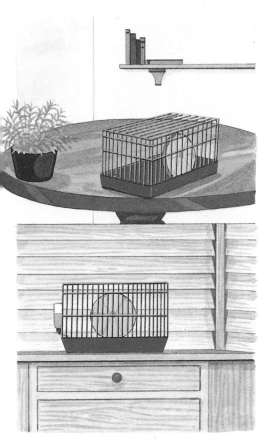

▲ Keep your hamster cage away from doors and windows, and raised off the ground. This will reduce the chances of your pet's escaping while you are cleaning out the cage. The top picture shows the cage on a table in the living room and the bottom picture shows the cage on a working surface in a shed.

►Hamsters enjoy climbing over the furniture. If you do allow your pet to roam free, stay near at hand in case it tries to escape. Make sure that doors and windows are closed, and that there are no gaps in the floorboards.

Cleaning and grooming

Hamsters **groom** and clean themselves, and you can sometimes watch them doing it. They need three things to keep their coats in good condition and to prevent them from becoming smelly — a good, well-balanced diet, enough exercise, and regular cleaning of their cages. The exceptions to this are the long-haired varieties, which need a light brushing and combing every day.

▲ The hamster larder is often hidden beneath wood shavings or straw. Do not disturb this except to remove moldy food or rotting greenstuff.

◄ Shorthaired hamsters are experts at grooming themselves as you can see from this picture. They do this very often to remove dust and scraps of food from their fur. They also have bouts of grooming activity, when faced with a new situation or problem.

One of the reasons for grooming pets, apart from keeping them clean, is so that you can check on the condition of their coats, eyes and mouths. With hamsters, you can do this in your daily 'playtime'. Watch for any sign of broken skin under the coat, runny eyes, or stains under the tail caused by **diarrhea**. Now and again check the teeth for color and condition. You can find out more about hamster health on pages 26 and 27.

Daily cleaning and care

You must set aside a few minutes each day for the daily cleaning jobs. Choose a time when your pet has finished eating. Take away the food bowl and wash it well. Empty the water container and fill it with fresh water. Make sure you do not spill any inside the cage. Check that the spout is within reach but not touching the litter. Remove droppings and any bits of food that have been left around.

Weekly cleaning

Once a week the cage needs a complete clean-out. You will need a hamster carrying cage or some other safe container while you do this. The hamster may be disturbed by the move, so keep your eye on it in case it tries to escape. Remove all the litter and bedding from the cage and throw it away. Check for damp patches before you put in the new litter and bedding. If there are any, clean them up and dry them thoroughly.

Do not disturb the larder more than you have to, but remove decaying food. When you have finished, return the hamster to its cage and stroke it for a while to make it feel safe. Finally — as always when you have been dealing with a pet — wash your hands.

▲ You should clean out your hamster's cage quite often. Sweep out the plastic tray so that all the old bedding and litter goes on to a large piece of paper. Your pet can watch from inside its cage while you are doing this job.

Hamster health care

You should give your hamster a proper diet, and cage it in a warm, dry place. Then it should live a healthy life of two years or more. Living on their own, hamsters do not risk picking up disease from other animals.

Signs of illness

You can easily check your hamster's health during the daily "playtime." The most common diseases are those listed on page 27. Others have to do with breathing and **digestion**.

Like other animals, hamsters clear dust from their noses by sneezing now and then. If your hamster continues to sneeze, there may be dust in the litter or bedding. Change these and the sneezing should stop.

Hamsters sometimes develop noisy, wheezy breathing. The cause may be dust or cold, damp air. Try moving the cage to a place where the air is warmer and drier.

▼ **In the wild, hamsters hibernate during the winter months and go to sleep. Your pet may go torpid if the temperature approaches freezing point. Do not try to wake it up but move the cage to a warmer place. Your pet will soon wake up and start moving around.**

▲ **Hamsters normally keep their incisor teeth short by constant gnawing. Should your pet's teeth become too long you must take it to the vet who will trim them down. Otherwise the hamster will have difficulty in feeding.**

Your pet's claws (left) may need trimming from time to time. Cut the nails straight across, without clipping too short. You can buy special clippers from the pet shop.

Diarrhea — runny droppings — is a common hamster problem. The most likely cause is rotten or moldy food that has been left in the cage. It is sometimes caused by a sudden change in diet. If your pet has diarrhea, take special care to keep the cage clean and change the litter often. The opposite condition — very hard droppings — is called **constipation**. The usual cause is lack of water or greenstuff.

Other dangers

Hamsters fall easily but they seldom harm themselves. After a bad fall, a hamster may lie still in a state of shock and appear to be dead. Put it back in its nesting box and leave it alone to recover. In an hour or two it will probably be back to normal.

In the wild, hamsters hibernate. Few pet hamsters do this, but in very cold weather your pet might go **torpid**, and curl up looking dead. If this should happen, try warming it in your hands, or take its cage into a warmer place and add some extra bedding. Let it come back to normal slowly.

Common hamster health problems		
Ailment	**Signs**	**What to do**
Abscess on body	Swelling from cut or scratch	Bathe with antiseptic until abscess breaks. Then clean pus away
Abscess in pouch	Caused by scratch from sharp piece of food. Swollen cheek, refusal to feed, runny eyes	Take to the vet as soon as possible
Colds and chills	Sneezing, refusal to feed, shivering	Keep warm. Take to vet if signs continue
Bald or thin coat		Check for **parasites**. If found, treat as below. If skin infected, consult vet
Parasites		Dust with an insect powder suitable for hamsters. Avoid getting powder in eyes
Wet tail	Serious diarrhea, refusal to eat, loss of condition	Take to vet at once, but wet tail is usually fatal. Burn all litter and bedding and disinfect cage before using again

Different colors

The golden hamsters of Syria were more reddish-brown than golden. They had whiter fur underneath and on their paws. But no two hamsters are exactly alike in coloring. By selective breeding from carefully chosen pairs, owners have produced hamsters with new coloring.

The new colors were strengthened by breeding from pairs in the same family. This is called **line breeding**. Color changes are brought about in a short time because hamsters breed so quickly.

Varieties of hamster with one overall color are called **self** varieties. Hamsters with different eye colors count as separate varieties. There are also many patterned varieties — banded, spotted and tortoiseshell. These patterns can be combined with any of the basic colors.

Cinnamon

Cinnamon

The Cinnamon has a light orange coat, with white underparts and paws. Its coloring has made it one of the favorite varieties in both Britain and the United States, where it was first introduced. The eye color is red. The clearest cinnamon color is seen on the cheeks.

Blond

Blond

The pale Blond hamster is one of the newer varieties, with an attractive creamy-fawn coat. It may have either red or black eyes, and the ears are pink.

Cream Banded

Banding is the most common of the coat patterns. Any of the color varieties can take the banded pattern. Sometimes the band goes all the way around the body, sometimes only part of the way around.

Cream Banded

Tortoiseshell

Smoke Pearl

▲ These are just a few of the many varieties of hamster. When you choose your pet, look at as many color varieties as you can. You will soon find that you have your own favorite color and coat.

Tortoiseshell

The tortoiseshell pattern (sometimes shortened to "tortie") is a mixture of different colors. By selective breeding, any color can be put into the tortoiseshell pattern.

Smoke Pearl

The Smoke Pearl hamster is pinkish-gray with black eyes and dark gray ears. It is one of the newer varieties and was bred to soften the dark gray color.

The color varieties	
Name	**Description**
Albino	White with dark ears
Albino, pink-eared	White with flesh-colored ears
Blond, black-eyed	Creamy fawn
Blond, red-eyed	Creamy fawn
Black	Brownish-black, darker at rear
Caramel	Reddish-brown
Chocolate	Dark brown, with lighter underparts
Cinnamon	Light orange, with white underparts
Cream, black-eyed	Apricot color
Cream, red-eyed	Apricot color or pale cream
Cream, ruby-eyed	Cream with pinkish tinge. Eye color darkens with age
Dove, black-eyed	Pale gray with a pink tinge
Dove, red-eyed	Pale gray with a pink tinge
Fawn, ruby eyed	Light brown
Golden, dark	Deep red-brown with dark patches around eyes
Golden, light	Light red-brown
Golden, normal	Reddish-brown with lighter underparts
Gray, dark	Dark gray with brownish tinge
Gray, dominant	Gray with flesh-colored tinge
Gray, light	Silvery gray
Honey	Golden honey-colored
Ivory, black-eyed	Cream colored
Ivory, red-eyed	Cream colored
Lilac	Pale gray with pink tinge
Piebald	White with equal patches of another color
Roan	Reddish-brown
Smoke Pearl	Pinkish-gray with darker cheeks
Sooty	Dark brownish-black
White, black-eyed	White, often with dark insides to ears
Yellow	Varies from apricot color to yellowish-cream

Note: Breeders are constantly introducing new color varieties. Others fall out of favor and some become extinct. This means that details of recognized varieties are likely to be changing all the time.

Different coats

The various colors described on the previous pages can be combined with different kinds of coats. This means that you can choose your pet hamster from a very wide range of varieties.

Longhairs, Satins and Rex

Longhairs — sometimes known as Angoras — have coats of fine hair which is usually thicker in males than in females. They can be bred in every color variety. If you are thinking of buying a longhaired hamster, beware! They need to be groomed every day with great care so the coat will not become matted. First the hair must be lightly brushed and then gently combed. Unless you are sure you will have time for this job day after day, it would be better to get a hamster with a standard coat.

Satins have glossy coats with the shiny look of silk. The fur is standard length. Satin-coated hamsters can groom themselves and they cause no extra work for their owners. But they must not be **paired** for breeding. This produces young with thin coats. The rule is to pair a satin parent with a standard-coated one.

▲ **Longhaired hamsters need to be groomed every day. The long hairs are very fine and soft. Brush gently down each side of the body. The hair will fall out if you treat it roughly.**

◄ **Satin-coated hamsters can groom themselves. Satins can have coats of any colors or markings. If two satins mate, their offspring will have very thin coats. It is best to mate a satin with a standard-coated hamster.**

There is another variety of golden hamster known as the Rex. There are also Rex cats and Rex rabbits. They all have shorthaired coats that will not lie flat but stand up rather like velvet. The whiskers of the Rex hamster are short and curly.

The Rex coat is curly and the Rex can be bred in any color. Breeders have found it hard to produce rex-coated hamsters with thick coats. Often, the result is a thin coat that looks rough instead of curly and sleek.

The hamster's coat

If your hamster is healthy and well cared for, the fur will feel like velvet to the touch. The color of your pet's coat and the quality of the fur are both things you can be proud of.

You can expect your hamster to live for 1½ to 2½ years, males often living longer than females. As a hamster grows older its coat will become thinner. Once the fur loses its quality the coat is unlikely to improve. There is little you can do about it, apart from giving your pet a warm, dry home and regular grooming.

▼ The coat of the Rex hamster does not lie flat and tends to stand up. The coat looks and feels like velvet or fine wool. Rex hamsters can be bred in many colors or markings.

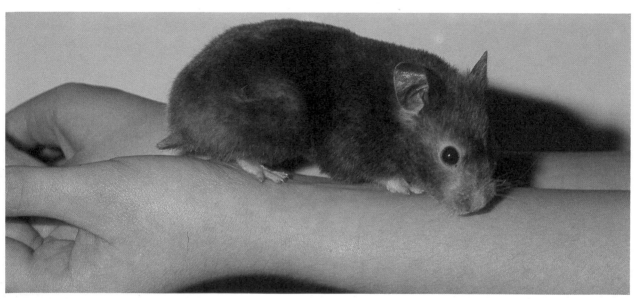

Other species of hamster

A fully grown hamster is usually about 10 cm (4 in) long from the tip of its nose to the end of its tail. There are numerous species of hamsters living in the wild, but most of them are unsuitable as pets.

The European hamster

The European hamster is one of the largest, growing to a length of about 15 cm (6 in). It is similar in appearance and coloring to the golden hamster, but it is fierce and cannot be tamed. When approached by another animal, such as the polecat, the European hamster screams and spits in its enemy's face. It is an **endangered species** and cannot be sold.

▼ The European hamster is very large and it is shaped like a guinea pig, with short legs and tail. These hamsters build their burrows near grain fields. They collect their food at night in their cheek pouches, taking grain back to their burrows. There they build up large stores of grain in the food chambers.

▲ The Chinese hamster has a grayish-brown coat with a darker line running from head to tail along the back. It has black ears and eyes and a white belly. Unlike golden hamsters, two or more Chinese hamsters can live in one cage.

The Korean gray hamster

Even larger is the Korean gray hamster, which can grow to a length of 20 cm (8 in). Although most species of hamster have hardly any tail at all, the Korean hamster may have a tail 5 cm (2 in) long. This animal has very large cheek pouches and is known to hoard huge stores of grain beneath the ground. At times of famine, Korean people have even used these stores to avoid starving. The Korean hamster is very rarely kept as a pet in captivity.

The Chinese hamster

Hamsters are by nature solitary animals and prefer to live on their own. Put two or more hamsters in the same cage and they will usually fight. There are, however, a few species of hamster that live in groups in the wild. The Chinese hamster is one of these social animals. Some pet shops now sell these little hamsters, which are only about half the size of a golden hamster. It is possible to keep two or more Chinese hamsters in the same cage, but they need careful watching. When the females are pregnant they are inclined to attack the males. Then they have to be split up and housed in separate cages.

The Russian hamster

The dwarf Russian hamster varies in size from 5 cm to 7 cm (2–3 in), only about half the size of the golden hamster, and is much easier to keep as a pet with others. These little animals come from a region where it snows all winter. As a result, their brownish-gray coats turn lighter as the weather gets cold. This is nature's way of protecting them from their enemies as they are difficult to see against the snowy background.

Showing hamsters

You have bought your hamster, looked after it well, and it is in fine condition. How does it compare with other hamsters? Is it the best hamster around?

In some countries you can put your hamster into a show. In Britain, for example, most towns have "fur and feather" shows with classes for hamsters, and they often have special classes for young owners. Shows and classes are advertised in British newspapers and posted in the public library. In many places there are Hamster Clubs where hamster owners can learn more about their hobby.

Perhaps you could organize a hamster club in your school or neighborhood and have your own hamster shows. This would be a good way to learn more about the various kinds of pet hamsters.

Preparing for a show

If you are going to show your hamster, you will need two special items of equipment. One is a show cage, or pen as it is called. This is a standard size and design, 20 cm × 15 cm × 15 cm (8 in × 6 in × 6 in). You will also need a travel box to carry your hamster to the show. This can be made of wood, with holes for **ventilation**. You must make sure that the door closes firmly.

A third special item — a grooming box — is useful. This contains fresh hay and sawdust, and the hamster is put into it for an hour or so each day to groom itself.

Besides keeping your hamster in top condition, the most important preparation for a show is getting your hamster used to its travel box and show cage, and to being handled by strangers. The show judge will take it out of the show cage for examination.

Hamster boxes

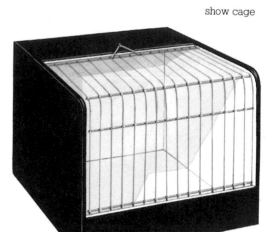
show cage

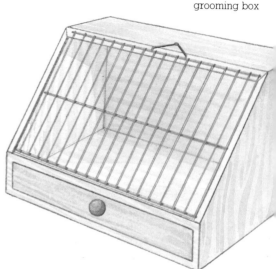
grooming box

travel box

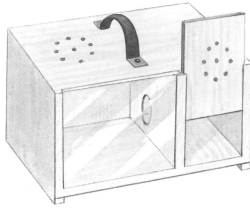

Judging

National hamster clubs have rules about how the different color varieties should look. Show judges follow these rules in awarding points. Whether you show your hamster or not, it is useful to obtain a copy of the **standard** for your color variety. Then you can find out whether your pet hamster is near show standard.

A typical hamster club points system

Points are deducted from 100 for the features listed below. This means that low scores in each category are good.

Feature	Points	Standard
Color and markings	30	As specified for the color variety
Type	15	Broad body, large head, blunt nose
Fur	15	Normal: short but dense and soft Longhairs: as specified for the coat type
Size	15	Large but no excess fat
Condition	15	Alert and fit; coat healthy
Eyes	5	Large but not protruding, set well apart
Ears	5	Large and erect

Further penalties of 5 points each may be deducted for excess fat, bones or nervousness.

▶ **A show judge in Britain is examining a hamster and calling off point deductions to his assistant. He will deduct points for any feature that fails to meet the required standard. The winning hamster in a category is the one with the lowest point score.**

Mating hamsters

Think carefully before you decide to try to breed hamsters. Remember that most owners keep only one hamster. If you decide to breed, you must be sure of finding good homes for each of the young, and arrange this in advance.

You must not use the home cage of the male or female for mating. You will need a special breeding cage. About a month after the young are born you will have to move them to a separate cage — or two cages if the litter is a large one. Think of all these things, and the cost of breeding, before making up your mind.

male

Male and female

It is easy to tell male and female hamsters apart. Gently turn the animal over, and, if it is a male, you will see, just behind the base of the tail, the swelling of the **testes**. Males can mate at any time after about six weeks, but they should not do so until they are three months old.

▼ If you want to breed hamsters, it is best to let the pair mate in territory which is new to both of them. They are less likely to fight. One way is to use a cage divided with a sheet of glass through which the two can get to know each other. In this photo, the female shows that she is willing by looking at the male through the glass.

▲ The female is placed in the male's part of the cage when she is ready to mate. Mating may last for some minutes. When it is finished, the hamsters should be put back in their own cages.

From about four or five weeks of age, the females come into **season** for about four hours every four days, in the evening. This is the only time they will mate. But it is hard to tell when a female is in season. For this reason, she must be introduced to the male for up to five evenings in a row.

Mating

The male is put into the breeding cage first, and then the female is introduced. She may start to fight, and if so she should be taken out at once. Gloves have to be worn to avoid being bitten or scratched.

If the female is willing to mate, she will face the male with a fixed stare. At the same time she curves her spine and raises her tail. Mating will soon follow and will continue for some minutes. When the male moves away from the female, he is picked up and returned to his own cage. If he stays, he may try to mate again and the female will attack him.

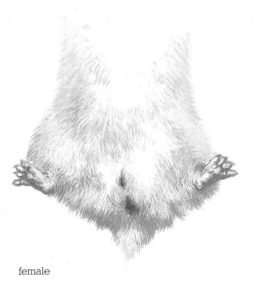

female

37

Pregnancy and birth

Once mating has taken place, the female should be settled in the cage where she is to stay until the birth of her litter. If the breeding cage is larger than her own cage, she can be left in it for her **pregnancy**. But it must contain a quiet, dark place where she can make her nest.

She should be disturbed as little as possible. If you have to handle her while you clean the cage, do so very carefully, using both hands.

The pregnant hamster

Remember that a litter will be born only sixteen days after mating. Seven or eight days after mating, the female will begin to look fatter than usual. Her stomach will get bigger each day. You should now start to increase her diet to include milk and high-energy foods such as oats, raisins and seeds.

Around the twelfth or thirteenth day, you should clean the cage and provide fresh litter and bedding. With this bedding, she will make her nest for the birth. From now on, you must not touch her until her young are about two weeks old. Keep an eye on her from a distance, and keep other members of the family away.

▲ You will soon be able to tell when the female is pregnant. After seven or eight days she will be much fatter as the baby hamsters begin to grow inside her. Now is the time to increase her food.

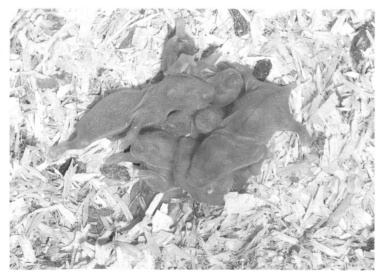

◄ Baby hamsters are born blind and without any fur. It is best to keep away from the cage in the early stages. Most of the time, the newborn hamsters will be covered by their mother, except when she goes to take food or water.

The birth

Hamsters give birth easily, usually late in the evening or during the night. The female will have her young in the nest she has made, and must not be disturbed. The act of giving birth makes hamsters nervous, and any disturbance may lead the mother to eat her young.

You will be impatient to see the litter and count them, but you must wait for about twelve days after birth. Then they will begin to explore outside the nest. Hamsters are born blind and without fur. The fur begins to grow after a few days. The eyes open when the young are ten to twelve days old. You must continue to provide the mother with extra food so that she can feed her young.

▼ It is not easy to tell how many babies there are in this litter. Seven or eight can be seen and there may be more. Most female hamsters have fourteen nipples. Litters of seventeen young have been known.

The young hamster family

The young hamsters emerge from the nest at about two weeks of age. You can enjoy watching them as they grow in size and become more adventurous. Your next task is to wean them. You have to get them to eat a solid diet instead of drinking their mother's milk. When this has been done, you must remove the young to their own cage.

Weaning

When they are old enough to explore the cage, the young will try any food they are offered. You can buy special meal at the pet shop. Cornflakes can be rolled out to make a fine powder. Brown bread can be soaked in a little milk and you can chop up greenstuff finely. These all make good "starter" foods.

Feed the young hamsters at a regular time, and clean up any mess afterward. Make sure that the mother also has plenty of food, as she will need to regain her strength.

▼ By the time the baby hamsters are seven days old, their fur will have grown. Their eyes will have begun to open. After a further seven days, their eyes will be fully open and they will be running about the cage.

▲ When the young hamsters are five or six weeks old they become very bouncy, and start sparring with each other. This soon turns into real fighting. Now is the time to sort out the males from the females, and hand over each of the young hamsters to their new owners.

Separation of litter

From about two to four weeks, the mother will live quite happily with her young and put up with their rough play. After that, she will get bored and may start to attack them. At about the same time, their rough play may turn into real fighting. You will have to keep a close watch at this time. At the first sign of trouble remove the young to their own cages.

Some breeders divide the sexes into separate cages right away. Others place the larger young in one cage and the smaller in another, so that the smaller hamsters have a fair share of the food. But after about six weeks males and females must be separated to keep them from mating. By ten weeks, at the latest, each hamster must have its own cage. By this time, the young should have gone to the new homes you have arranged for them.

Separation of the sexes is very important. If you do not do it in time, you could have a "population explosion" on your hands!

41

Raising hamsters as a hobby

Most people who own hamsters have only one, or perhaps two. If you become really interested, you may want to have more. If so, you will need a "hamstery" for them. The ideal hamstery would be a backyard shed fitted out like the one shown on these pages.

What you would need

The shed should be fitted out with shelves. These would have to be wide enough for the hamster cages and, if you plan to breed, for the larger breeding cages. The windows and door must fit tightly so that there are no drafts.

The shed will need an electricity supply. Then you can use greenhouse heaters to keep an even temperature in the winter. You will need lighting so that you can attend to the hamsters in the winter evenings. A low light kept on overnight in the winter will help to prevent your hamsters from becoming torpid.

If you plan to show your hamsters, it helps to have a bench at table height. Then you can inspect them and prepare their show cages. There should be adequate storage space for grooming materials, water bottles and spare cage toys. Dry foods and bedding materials should be stored in metal tins and bins with tightly-fitting lids.

The shed must be kept well aired. In warm, sunny weather the outer door can be left open. But the fine-mesh inner door must be kept closed at all times to keep out cats, rats and mice. There should be enough space on the shelves for a sufficient gap to be left between cages.

Before you decide to raise a number of hamsters, you might want to start a local hamster club. Then you could exchange ideas with other owners and learn from them.

▶ **Most people just have one or possibly two hamsters as pets in the home. There are, however, some people for whom hamsters become a lifetime hobby. If there is a shed in the backyard, they convert this into a "hamstery." The one in the picture is large enough to house twelve hamsters or even more. Each animal has its own cage.**

The hamster food and litter is stored in metal or plastic bins. Food must not be spilt on to the floor as this will attract rats and mice. In warm weather, the main door is left open, but the wire door must be kept firmly closed. Doors and windows must fit very tightly so that small field mice cannot get in through the cracks.

Backyard shed used as a hamstery

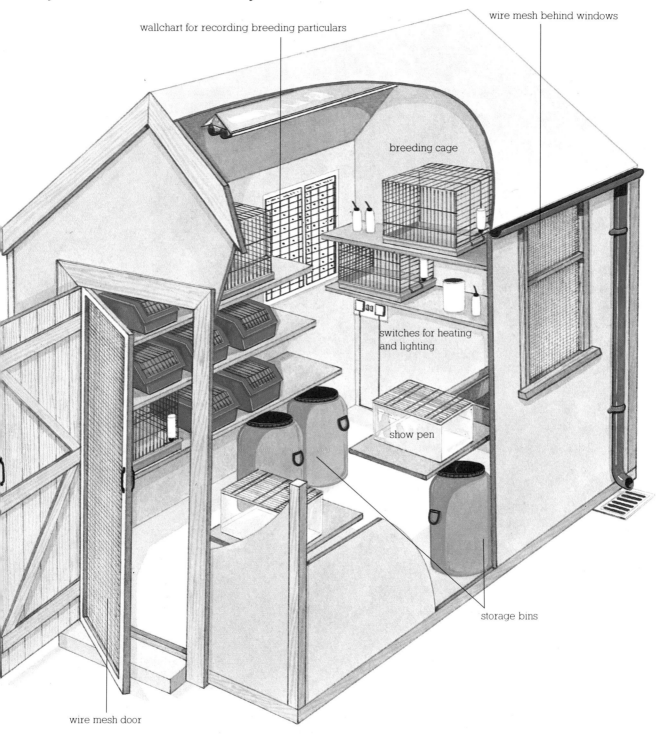

wallchart for recording breeding particulars

wire mesh behind windows

breeding cage

switches for heating and lighting

show pen

storage bins

wire mesh door

Glossary

aggressive: always ready to quarrel or attack

burrow: a hole in the ground made by an animal as its home

constipation: stomach upset which causes hard droppings

diarrhea: stomach upset which causes loose, runny droppings

diet: the kinds of food usually eaten by an animal

digestion: the process by which an animal converts food to energy

endangered species: a kind of animal in danger of dying out or becoming extinct. The giant panda is an endangered species

groom: to clean and tidy the coat

herbivore: an animal that eats plants

hibernate: to sleep through the winter months

hygiene: cleanliness

incisor: a sharp, chisel-shaped tooth at the front of the mouth, used for gnawing

instinct: natural behavior that does not have to be learned

line-breeding: breeding from members of the same family

litter: (1) the young hamsters resulting from one mating (2) sawdust or other material used to cover the cage floor

pairing: matching male and female hamsters from one mating

parasite: an animal such as an insect that lives on the body of another animal

pregnancy: the state or condition of a female when a baby is growing inside her body

rodent: an animal that gnaws and nibbles with its front teeth

season: the period when a female can be mated

selective breeding: breeding from a carefully selected male and female to produce young with certain looks and qualities

self: one overall color

solitary: living alone

standard: rules laid down for judging hamsters of particular color or coat varieties

testes: male organs which hold sperm

torpid: in a state of deep sleep

ventilation: causing air to move around freely

Further reading

Gerbil Pets and Other Small Rodents by Ray Broekel. Childrens Press, 1983.

Hamsters by Helga Fritzsche. Barron's Educational Series, Inc., 1982.

Hamsters by Fiona Henrie. Franklin Watts, 1981.

Hamsters: All About Them by Alvin and Virginia Silverstein. Lothrop, Lee and Shepard, 1974.

Hamsters, Gerbils, Guinea Pigs, Pet Mice and Pet Rats by James and Lynn Hahn, Franklin Watts, 1977.

The Life of a Hamster by Jan Feder. Childrens Press, 1982.

Pets by Frances N. Chrystie. Little, Brown, 1974.

Taking Care of Your Hamster by Joyce Pope. Franklin Watts, 1986.

Index